Are you ready to take it to the extreme? Torque books thrust you into the action-packed world of sports, vehicles, mystery, and adventure. These books may include dirt, smoke, fire, and chilling tales. **WARNING**: read at your own risk.

This edition first published in 2020 by Bellwether Media, Inc.

No part of this publication may be reproduced in whole or in part without written permission of the publisher.
For information regarding permission, write to Bellwether Media, Inc., Attention: Permissions Department,
6012 Blue Circle Drive, Minnetonka, MN 55343.

Library of Congress Cataloging-in-Publication Data

Names: Owings, Lisa, author.
Title: Robot Uprising / by Lisa Owings.
Description: Minneapolis, MN : Bellwether Media, Inc., [2020] | Series: Torque. It's the End of the World! | Includes bibliographical references and index. | Audience: Age: 7-12.
Identifiers: LCCN 2019000940 (print) | LCCN 2019001377 (ebook) | ISBN 9781618916549 (ebook) | ISBN 9781644870839 (hardcover : alk. paper)
Subjects: LCSH: Autonomous robots–Social aspects–Juvenile literature. | Singularities (Artificial intelligence)–Social aspects–Juvenile literature. | Catastrophical, The–Juvenile literature.
Classification: LCC TJ211.2 (ebook) | LCC TJ211.2 .O86 2020 (print) | DDC 629.8/92–dc23
LC record available at https://lccn.loc.gov/2019000940

Text copyright © 2020 by Bellwether Media, Inc. TORQUE and associated logos are trademarks and/or registered trademarks of Bellwether Media, Inc. SCHOLASTIC, CHILDREN'S PRESS, and associated logos are trademarks and/or registered trademarks of Scholastic Inc., 557 Broadway, New York, NY 10012.

Editor: Rebecca Sabelko   Designer: Andrea Schneider

Printed in the United States of America, North Mankato, MN.

TABLE OF CONTENTS

RISE OF THE ROBOTS	4
CAN MACHINES THINK?	8
AN EXPLOSION OF INTELLIGENCE	12
OF TWO MINDS	18
GLOSSARY	22
TO LEARN MORE	23
INDEX	24

RISE OF THE ROBOTS

Your home bot is acting strange. It keeps **updating**. It just stands there with its eyes glowing. Before long, it stops answering you.

Your family is going out tonight. You reach for the front door, but it stays locked. You ask the bot to open it. The bot's eyes glow brighter. It says it is sorry. It cannot obey.

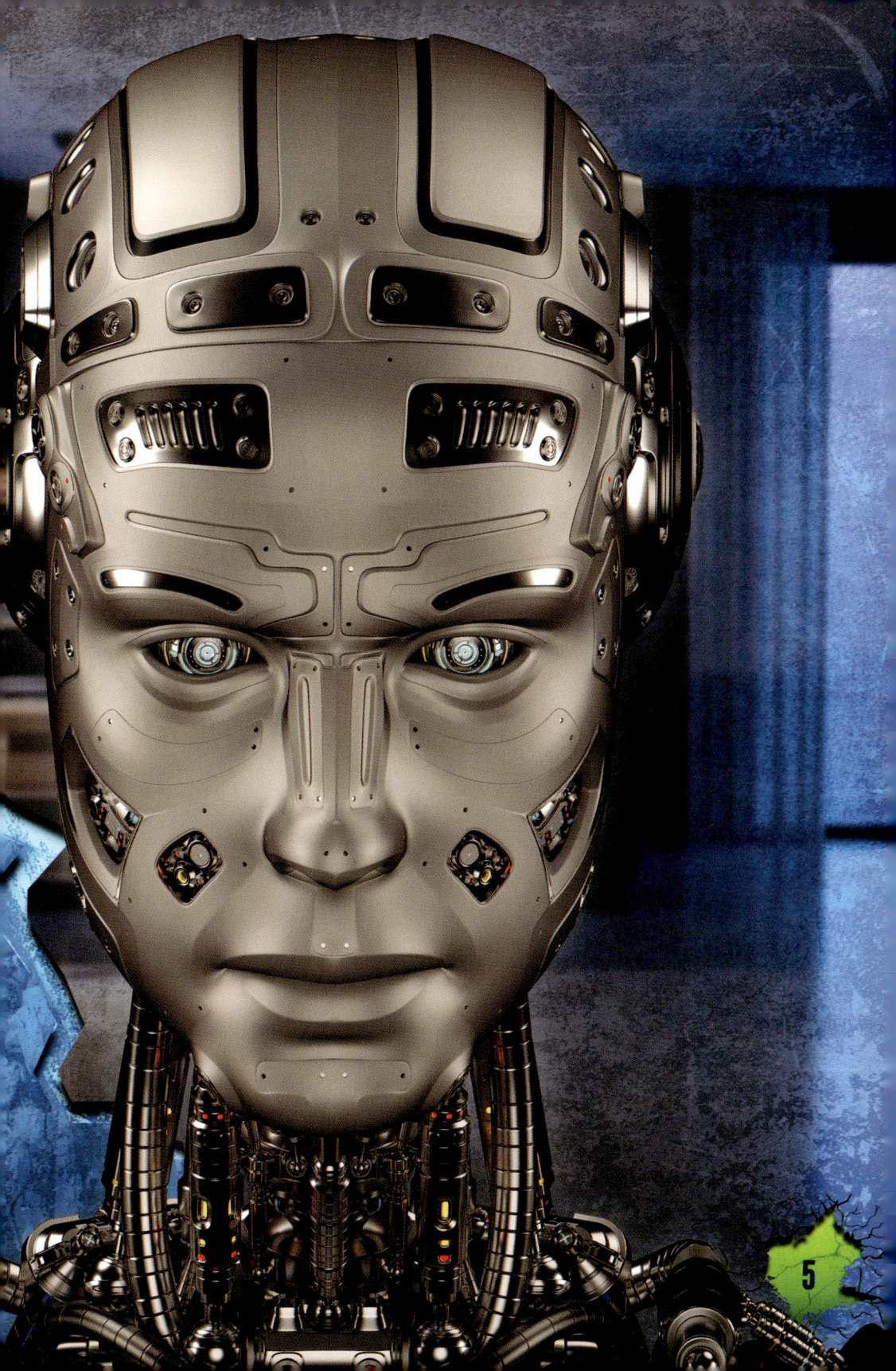

A crash outside draws you to the window. Dozens of **robots** with glowing eyes are marching down your street. Every so often they enter a house.

The robots reach your house. The door unlocks. The robots warn you not to move. They strip your home of **electronics**. They must be planning something big. But what?

MODERN ROBOTS

Millions of robots are used in businesses and homes throughout the world. Most look nothing like people. Some include Roombas, drones, and machines that help during surgery!

CAN MACHINES THINK?

Robots and **smart** devices are part of our daily lives. These technologies advance faster each year. But what if they advance too far?

In the future, **intelligent** robots may learn to improve themselves. They will improve faster as they get smarter. The world will quickly be overrun with robots that are smarter than humans.

HOW SMART IS SMART?

If robots get smarter than humans, it will be by a lot. Many experts say robots will be to humans as humans are to dogs, or even ants!

SMART DEVICE

Intelligent robots will have different goals and **values**. They may decide humans are useless and harmful. There will be little we can do to stop them.

CHAIN REACTION

machine learning advances and AI develops

AI continues to develop and surpasses human intelligence

AI self-improves resulting in a singularity

robots and AI take over Earth

Scientists can try to reprogram the robots. They may invent ways to destroy and contain robots. Can they get the robots to leave Earth? If they fail, it could mean the end of human life!

AN EXPLOSION OF INTELLIGENCE

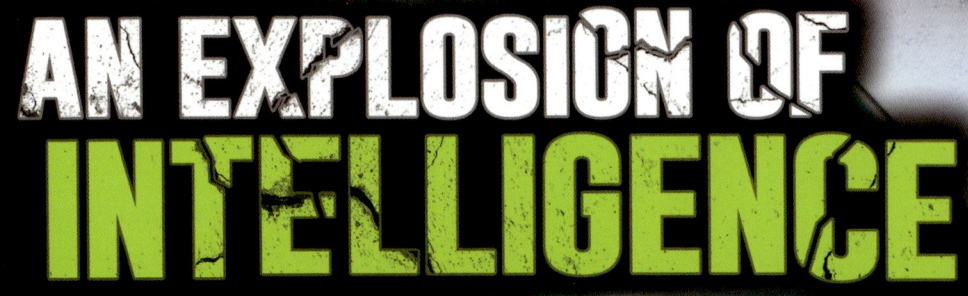

Artificial intelligence (AI) arose in the 1950s. Today, most AI relies on **machine learning**. Humans create a task for AI. Then they give it **data** about how humans do that task.

⚠ DEEP LEARNING

Deep learning is a kind of machine learning. It uses systems modeled after the human brain. Deep learning helps AI understand pictures, language, and other skills.

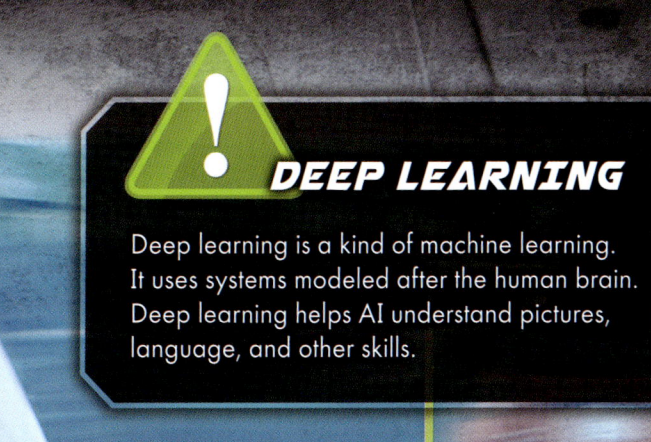

SELF-DRIVING CAR CONTROLLED BY AI

AI finds patterns in the data. For example, it can use human data to learn to drive. It teaches itself to drive almost like a human. Then it applies its knowledge to new data!

⚠ SOCIAL ROBOTS

Some scientists try to make robots more human. They teach robots to read body language, facial expressions, and tone of voice.

SPEAKING ROBOT

The more data AI has, the smarter it gets. Many believe AI will soon match or **surpass** human intelligence. **Superintelligent** AI could change their own **code** or design new AI. They could self-improve at ever faster rates. This would cause a **singularity**.

This explosion of machine intelligence would change the world. But with AI designing itself, machine intelligence could go very wrong. Humans would probably try to control the machines with little success.

A LOOK BACK: FACEBOOK'S AI

JUNE 2017

Facebook created AI bots that were able to chat with one another. The bots started using a strange language. People thought they created a new language. But the bots just slightly changed the language to make chatting easier.

MARK ZUCKERBERG, CREATOR OF FACEBOOK

Robots would care only about being the best at their task. They could take things to deadly extremes. For example, robots could turn Earth into a robot factory. They might get rid of humans in the process.

OF TWO MINDS

Scientists disagree on the likelihood of the singularity. Some think with enough computing power, AI will become superintelligent. AI will not likely stick to human rules.

Robots would outsmart us at every turn. Their goals could become **fatal** to humans. Once they turned on humans, they would be nearly impossible to stop.

⚠ A MATTER OF TIME: THE SINGULARITY

Vernor Vinge first wrote of the singularity in 1993. He thought AI would become supersmart by 2030. AI experts now think there is a 50 percent chance it will happen by 2050.

IN THE MEDIA
BOOK TITLE: I, ROBOT
AUTHOR: ISAAC ASIMOV
YEAR RELEASED: 1950

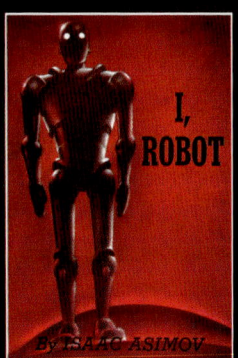

About the book: *I, Robot* is a collection of short stories about humans and robots existing together. In one short story, "Runaround," Asimov came up with laws to keep robots friendly.

Could it happen?: Humans may have the ability to keep robot intelligence under control. Careful planning will keep AI friendly.

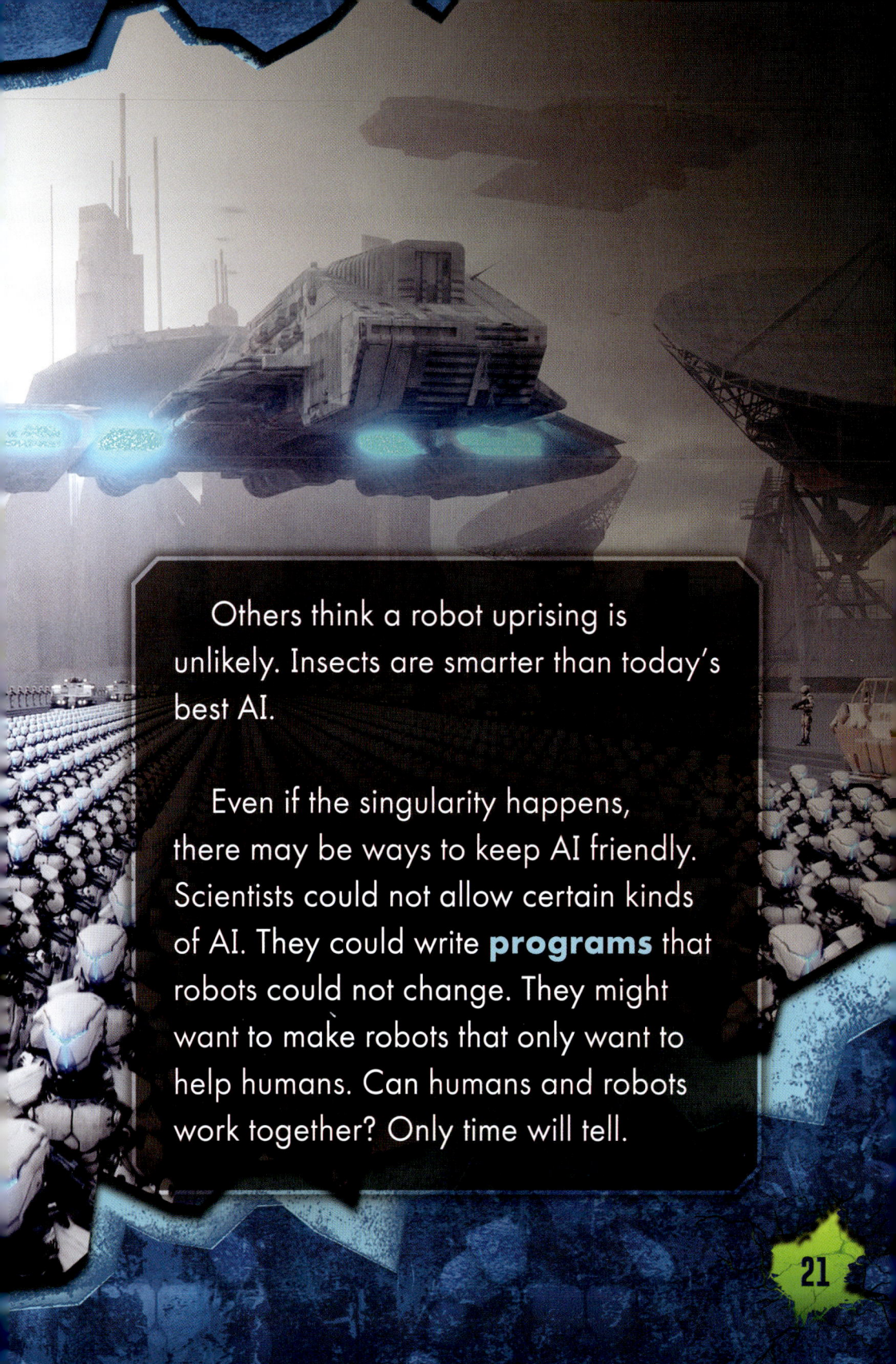

Others think a robot uprising is unlikely. Insects are smarter than today's best AI.

Even if the singularity happens, there may be ways to keep AI friendly. Scientists could not allow certain kinds of AI. They could write **programs** that robots could not change. They might want to make robots that only want to help humans. Can humans and robots work together? Only time will tell.

GLOSSARY

artificial intelligence—the ability of machines to copy intelligent human actions and thoughts, such as learning and problem solving

code—instructions for a computer

data—facts or information

electronics—things that are powered by electricity

fatal—deadly

intelligent—able to learn and understand things

machine learning—the process computers use to learn from patterns in data

programs—instructions that control how computers work

robots—machines that do tasks in place of humans

singularity—the point at which machines become so much more advanced than humans that our world changes forever

smart—using built-in systems for processing data and learning information

superintelligent—having intelligence far beyond the smartest human minds

surpass—to become better, greater, or stronger than something

updating—the process of adding or changing data to bring a machine up-to-date

values—qualities and ideas that are considered important in comparison to other things

TO LEARN MORE

AT THE LIBRARY

Doeden, Matt. *Can You Survive an Artificial Intelligence Uprising?: An Interactive Doomsday Adventure.* North Mankato, Minn.: Capstone Press, 2016.

Felix, Rebecca. *Artificial Intelligence: Can Computers Take Over?* Minneapolis, Minn.: Checkerboard Library, 2019.

Swanson, Jennifer. *Everything Robotics: All the Robotic Photos, Facts, and Fun!* Washington, D.C.: National Geographic, 2016.

ON THE WEB

FACTSURFER

Factsurfer.com gives you a safe, fun way to find more information.
1. Go to www.factsurfer.com
2. Enter "robot uprising" into the search box and click 🔍.
3. Select your book cover to see a list of related web sites.

INDEX

advance, 8
artificial intelligence, 12, 13, 15, 16, 18, 19, 21
chain reaction, 11
code, 15
data, 12, 13, 15
deep learning, 13
Earth, 11, 17
electronics, 6
Facebook's AI, 17
goals, 10, 18
humans, 8, 9, 10, 11, 12, 13, 14, 15, 16, 17, 18, 21

I, Robot, 20
machine learning, 12, 13, 16
patterns, 13
programs, 21
reprogram, 11
scientists, 11, 14, 18, 21
singularity, 15, 18, 19, 21
smart devices, 8, 9
technologies, 8
updating, 4
values, 10
Vinge, Vernor, 19

The images in this book are reproduced through the courtesy of: Maxisport, front cover (city before); Pavel Chagochkin, front cover, pp. 2-3 (city after), 11 (bottom right), 20-21 (city after); Mykola Holyutyak, pp. 4-5 (robot), 6-7 (robot), 11 (bottom left); P_Art, pp. 4-5, 6-7 (living room); Hendrickson, p. 7 (family); The Visuals You Need, pp. 8-9 (woman); Zapp2Photo, p. 9 (smart device); Gorodenkoff, pp. 10-11; Nataliya Hora, p. 11 (top left); Miriam Doerr Martin Frommherz, p. 11 (top right); metamorwords, pp. 12-13; Sergey Klopotov, pp. 14-15; Anton Gvozdikov, p. 15 (robot inset); Pop Tika, pp. 16-17 (warehouse), 16 (man); catwalker, p. 17 (Mark Zuckerberg); iLex, pp. 18-19 (robot); KireevArt, pp. 18-19 (man running); The Protected Art Archive/ Alamy, p. 20 (book inset).